Try Jesus

Try Jesus

Begin Your Walk in Truth

Kenyatta Jensen

© 2010 by Kenyatta Jensen. All rights reserved.
2nd Printing 2014.

Trusted Books is an imprint of Deep River Books. The views expressed or implied in this work are those of the author. To learn more about Deep River Books, go online to www.DeepRiverBooks.com.

No part of this publication may be reproduced, stored in a retrieval system or transmitted in any way by any means—electronic, mechanical, photocopy, recording or otherwise—without the prior permission of the Publisher, except as provided by USA copyright law.

Unless otherwise noted, all Scriptures are taken from the *Holy Bible, New International Version®, NIV®*. Copyright © 1973, 1978, 1984 by Biblica, Inc.™ Used by permission of Zondervan. All rights reserved worldwide.

Scripture references marked kjv are taken from the *King James Version* of the Bible.

ISBN 13: 978-1-63269-181-1
Library of Congress Catalog Card Number: 2009906741

To Jordan, Noah, Elli, Elijah, Isaiah, Danielle, and Amadis, the next generation; as Mom I may fail you, but God never will. As God teaches, molds, and equips you, go and tell of His goodness.

Contents

Acknowledgments	ix
Preface	xi
Chapter One: Living in Darkness	1
Chapter Two: Becoming a Light	13
Chapter Three: A Whole New You	19
Chapter Four: Talking to God	25
Chapter Five: Trials and Tribulations	31
Chapter Six: Surrendering	37
Chapter Seven: Knowing God's Word	43
Chapter Eight: Hearing God's Voice	49
Chapter Nine: The War	53
Chapter Ten: Why Me?	59
Chapter Eleven: Adjusting Your Life	67

Acknowledgments

FIRST, THANK YOU, God, for always being at work in my life. Thank You for giving me the privilege of serving You by helping others in this way. May it ultimately serve to build Your kingdom.

While I was writing this book, one stumbling block after another occurred. The last one involved my losing the only manuscript I had of this book due to multiple viruses found on my laptop. It was surreal, yet not surprising.

Dan, thank you so much for your support and patience as I was writing this book. Thanks for dedicating hours of your time to retrieving most of what I lost and for rebuilding my laptop. You've got skills! Even though we began our journey like the foolish man who built his house upon the sand, I have truly experienced God in and during our marriage. We couldn't have come this far without Him. As my husband, thank you for all of your sacrifices—for every little one and especially for every big one. Thank you for being an awesome father. I am blessed. I love you.

Preface

Dear heavenly Father,

I am so glad to have You as a part of my life. You are a transforming God, and You are glorious in every way. It is with You that I have found strength. Thank You for convicting my heart, delivering me out of the wilderness, and restoring my spirit. You have created in me a new heart. Please continue to fill me with Your Spirit and direct my paths, in the name of Jesus. Allow me to hear Your voice and have the discerning spirit to know when You speak. I desire to be obedient to Your will for my life, that Your glory will shine through me. Remind me to offer my body as a living sacrifice to You each day. I praise You and exalt You for who You are. May this book be used for Your glory. You are so worthy of my praise. Amen.

THIS BOOK IS written in honor of my heavenly Father and to share with you, simply from one ordinary person to another, what God has taught me through my Lord and Savior, Jesus Christ. I desire to provide hope to those who do not understand the purpose of their journey and who therefore feel as if they are stuck in a struggle to change the course of their lives.

I write with my own journey in mind. Like many, I have walked through the wilderness blinded by the darkness. Thoughts of pleasing and serving the Lord with my life were voided from my mind. On the contrary, I went with the flow in life. What felt good became good. This happened until my lack of purpose became evident to me. When I called on the Lord, He heard and delivered me. Now I believe in His purpose for my life.

During my younger years, I had an intensely self-sufficient personality. Experiences in my life went hand in hand with my individual thought processes. I depended on what *I* thought, what *I* wanted, and what *I* felt. Experiences constructed the walls of fear, resentment, and anger in my heart. Behind these walls I was protected and I felt safe, yet there was no peace. My experiences took me down several paths, and as I walked in darkness, I stayed in the wilderness. With the help of God, I now know that my choices exemplified what my relationship with Jesus was like.

My exposure to church was occasional growing up. I never entered a church with my entire family. Most of my exposure took place when my mother sent my brother and me to church on a bus that came through our neighborhood. It was during one of those Sundays that I remember asking the Lord to come into my heart. Although the youth pastor said that the Lord will never leave me and that I did not have to ask Him again to come into my heart, I would ask over and over, not understanding what the youth pastor meant or even if he was right in what he told us. I remember that I certainly did not want him to be wrong, because in my childlike way, I really wanted the Lord to come into my heart.

During my senior year of high school, I attended church with a friend and her family. Still, my understanding of salvation was only slightly impacted. Then as a young adult in college, I believed in Jesus, but I in no way understood what it meant to have Jesus as Lord of my life. Jesus did not truly become Lord of my life until I became an adult, after I was married.

Preface

The Bible tells us that "all have sinned and fall short of the glory of God" (Romans 3:23). Yet, He can take anyone of us and shine through our sins. I am a living example of how the power of God can transform a person. I will never be joyful about the sins in my life, but I will forever be shameless regarding God's glory in my life.

You might believe there is a God. You even might have heard of His Son, Jesus, and asked Him to come into your life. Or you might have been deterred from wanting to know much at all about Jesus due to a tragedy or to watching the walk of professing Christians. I was once there. Along my journey, however, there finally came a point when I learned the principle of allowing Jesus to be Lord of my life. I now know that your purpose is found and your deepest needs are met in Him.

As you read this book, consider the material presented as it applies to you before moving on to the next chapter. I encourage you to examine your relationship with Jesus and how it has been portrayed in your decisions, actions, attitudes, and relationships. Then, if you have not already, consider trying Jesus.

—Kenyatta Jensen
Dixon, California
June 2008

Chapter One

Living in Darkness

In him was life, and that life was the light of men.
—John 1:4

AS YOU AND I experience this journey called life, we share a basic need—the need to know who we are and why we are here. We've all observed people who seem to grasp their purpose in life. But many people, although appearing to be quite well adjusted, desire, to some degree at least, to be delivered from the familiar darkness of meaningless living. Still others show no interest in finding the light of purpose and are content to wander aimlessly through life.

In any case, God, who designed and created us with reason, is both our purpose and the gateway to living out that purpose. Consequently, we must get to know our Creator if we want to discover—through a relationship with Jesus—why we were put on this earth.

Sadly, many people live in darkness, in bondage, because the environment in which they live provides no vision. Whether rich or poor, privileged or underprivileged, without a relationship with Jesus, we cannot see the entrapments of worthlessness, hopelessness, selfishness, resentment, deceit, confusion, vengeance, and lust. But in Jesus "was life, and that life was the light of men. The light shines in the darkness, but the darkness has not understood it" (John 1:4–5). Experiencing salvation through Jesus changes everything, but getting to that point of saying "yes" to Him isn't always easy.

There was a time when I was hesitant and maybe even scared to turn my life over to God. I thought I had to become perfect before coming to the Lord. Since I knew that would take a miracle, I didn't dare make a move. The standard of perfection, like Jesus, didn't seem attainable. I thought the perfect time for Jesus to deal with me would be on my deathbed. Under those circumstances, I had less chance of making a mistake. I didn't want to become a follower of Jesus and then fail the Lord.

I was concerned about becoming like other Christians I had met. It seemed as though Christians often criticized others in a manner that portrayed an inability to relate to either wrong behavior or a person who had acted wrongly. This general sense, along with several experiences, helped to reinforce my lack of interest in surrendering to Christ. I had heard—and later came to know—that Jesus loves sinners no matter what they've done, but my experiences were not of love.

I remember a time when a Chamorro friend of mine, with whom I'd go to the club, wanted my opinion about the number of men she'd had sex with. She said, "Kenyatta, I've been thinking. I have a child, and I'm not even in a committed relationship. I've had sex with fourteen men. Do you think that's too many?"

I told her it was good she was thinking about such things and that she should really consider slowing down.

Later, I told a Christian friend what was confided to me in order to get his perspective, and what spilled out of his mouth truly rubbed me the wrong way. "What is she, a slut?" he blurted out.

My gut wrenched. I was hurt by his response, because (little did he know) my list was no better. She obviously did not feel good about her behavior and was beginning to question her actions. I had begun fiddling with those same thoughts regarding my own actions. The love she sought in the arms of those men and the burden of leaving empty-handed was familiar to me.

On another occasion, I had a relationship with a Christian who, because we were sexually active, acted as if he didn't know me on Sundays. Sundays were set aside for him to go to church. He consented to sex any day of the week except Sundays, and to ensure this, I would either leave his apartment early on Sunday mornings after staying the night and studying on Saturday, or we would just schedule around Sunday. I thought his behavior was hypocritical, but pride seemed to lift him up when he explained his behavior to me. I thought I was at least being honest with myself concerning the authentic me. Christian or not, I could see no difference between his walk and mine.

In my early adult years, I was judged, ostracized, and called names by devout Christians because of the choices I made. Although God has been the reconciling force in our relationship today, it was my initial relationship with a special friend and loved one that in some ways confirmed, and in others confused, my views about Christians. At the time, the fact that she had been a pastor's wife for many years made a difference in my expectations. Due to my ignorance, I had certain expectations of her that I would not necessarily have had for someone else. I thought that having been married to a pastor she would have known the Bible quite well. Therefore, I expected her to be kinder and more compassionate than most people. Not only did she fail to meet my faulty expectations, but she showed me a side of her that held such staunch judgment of others. In some ways this magnified my reasoning as to why I did not want to adapt to a Christian lifestyle.

Let me mention that I chose to enter into a marriage that was in no way grounded on biblical principles. As a result, I experienced disapproval. Once, this loved one called and wouldn't say hello, but instead ignored me if I answered the telephone. As I addressed her behavior, she'd scream and rage until I hung up. The vileness with which she once yelled, "Home wrecker!" was something I had only seen on television shows during attacks pertaining to racial injustice and inequality. Then when she said, "I forgive you," the harshness of her tone stifled any possibility of sincerity. As I listened, I experienced the kind of sound that personified the word *hatred*. It was unlike anything I'd known before. Nothing had ever brought me to confront another person so boldly, with such energy and criticism, so I couldn't understand her audacity. I could see she was trying to make me feel rotten because of my worldly state, but I suppressed any feelings of remorse while under attack and stood my ground. I only saw what I thought was one of the meanest people I had ever encountered.

As time progressed, I became pregnant with twins. At five months, I went into labor and was admitted to the hospital for four days and three nights. The doctor was able to slow my contractions, but they gradually sped up again. I opted to discontinue the painful steroid shots that aided in strengthening the babies' lungs and to allow God to have His way.

I left the hospital in tears, fearing for the premature delivery of my twins. When I arrived at home, I wrote a letter to this person, because I didn't want our differences to be the cause of my not informing her of the babies' health should God decide to take them home. I thought regardless of our differences that life and death mattered.

Sadly, no interest or concern was shown and she didn't respond to my letter. (This type of behavior continued through the birth of my next child.) God, however, knew what was to come. He entrusted me with beautiful, healthy boys, for whom I am so thankful. God tugged at my heart and gave me the will to embrace this person in such a special way when she wanted to become involved with my family. Although the yelling and name calling ceased, her mindset could just as easily be understood through her actions. While many of her actions were the source of confusion for my family, God gave me the restraining tongue I needed when I witnessed unbecoming behavior. He helped me choose the best words when I addressed her behavior and gave me the wisdom to dare to implement appropriate boundaries.

The journey began as a painful one, and although she didn't seem to see in herself the degree of "sin" she was able to point out in someone "like me," God did soothe my pain. In many ways embracing her has been a blessing. I can look up at God, close my eyes, and nod knowing He knew the specific areas in my character He was giving me the opportunity to build when He allowed my path to cross this loved one's path. She became an active and enthusiastic part of my family, bringing hundreds of smiles to my children's faces. I would be misleading you if I said that we now have the ideal relationship, but after getting to know her and hearing some of her unfortunate experiences, I've come to understand some of her actions towards me—not that I agree with them, but I can certainly understand them. After seeking for God's handprint in her design, I have found much to be thankful for in her.

Unfortunately, such observations and experiences quietly impacted me. In many ways I thought I was better off staying as I was rather than becoming like some of the professing Christians I'd witnessed. My childhood standard of just making it to heaven seemed like enough. I did not see a reason to draw closer to Jesus or to live like a Christian. I've realized that when we are living in darkness sometimes the only Jesus a person sees is the Jesus in a Christian. Therefore, as a Christian, it is important how we treat others. When Jesus is present in a person's life, the experiences of others around that person should be met with some measure of love, something we all crave. But somehow many of us become discombobulated over what love is—we don't feel it and we don't see it.

When I was a child, I witnessed countless fights and arguments in my enviroment. A few times when knives were drawn and fights really got out of control, the police appeared and calmed my surroundings, which sometimes looked like the aftermath of a tornado. During the fights, my brother and I would shut ourselves in a room and cry together or crawl under the bed for safety. By the time I was in high school, I became fed up with the fights, and knew I needed to leave once I graduated.

As a teenager I had been sexually violated, but at the time I didn't know what sexual abuse encompassed. All I had were my feelings that something wasn't right. Occasionally, I was violated in another way. When I was held down, I'd hear laughter, as if we were playing a hilarious game, and the next thing I knew a finger would manage to get stuck in my rectum and sometimes I was forced to smell it. Yeah, I know, gross. This was nothing short of intrusive and my feelings were steadily becoming explosive.

At seventeen, the driving force in my life was my desire for independence. Under no circumstances did I wish to return. I told myself that I was a survivor and that I would take care of myself.

When I entered my independence I longed for a love that was unfamiliar to me. I longed for love that would not eventually hurt me and for acceptance that was unconditional. I looked forward to having a "home sweet home" someday, shared with a man who would love and protect me.

Throughout my college years, I continued on what seemed like a scavenger hunt for what I longed for. The love of a man was the best kind of love I knew. I missed seeing my need for a relationship with Jesus as I watched others and as I relied on myself. It wasn't until after I married that I turned to the Lord with a will to hand over my ways. He was my last hope amid the mess I had created.

After all my experiences, I have now resolved that we can observe Christians as a model for behavior, but no one is perfect. Jesus is the ultimate model and standard of perfection. He modeled for us an intimate relationship with God the Father.

Shortly after I decided to seek a relationship with the Lord, I shared with a neighbor what Christ was teaching me. I said, "Girl, this class I'm taking at church is opening my eyes to so many things. It breaks things down to my level. I never knew the reason why people should go to church. I just figured I could read my Bible at home if I wanted to. I didn't need a church for that. I'm learning that I not only receive life lessons in church, but I'm also in an atmosphere to give to God. Not only that, but I've learned that when I'm by myself, I'm weaker. By being with other people who want to live their lives for God, I grow by seeing what God is doing in and through their lives."

"That's all fine for you," she replied. "But I'm afraid to get to know the Lord."

"Why?"

"I heard that if I do, the devil will come after me, and I don't need any more problems."

It amazed me how matter-of-factly she stated this, but I understood what she thought she was saying.

"Well, as a matter of fact, the devil *is* after you," I replied, "and you're already making him happy by not seeking a relationship with the Lord. Personally, I'm afraid to live without the Lord, because I know what He's done in my life. I've been through so many things I couldn't have handled without Him, and I'm sure I'll face plenty of other things only He can get me through."

I don't know if I succeeded, but I wanted to convey that without Him, *I* cannot—period.

My neighbor said, "Well, one thing that really bothers me about going to church is that churches always want your money. I work too hard for what I have to be giving it to some church."

"I hear you. I completely understand what you're saying, because I felt the same way. But one thing I'm learning is that I'm not going to understand everything God desires of me. I learned that obedience is better than sacrifice. I give money out of thankfulness and obedience to please God, not because I feel like giving away money that I can use. I don't know how to describe it, but what I'm learning makes me look at things differently."

About a year and a half later, the same woman excitedly approached me to tell me about how someone had sent her some Scripture-based material during a time when she had difficulty finding a job. Her excitement came from having been uplifted by a certain scripture.

"Ken, guess what!" she said, crossing the street. "I've been feeling so depressed lately, wondering why no one is hiring me. Then out of nowhere I received this book in the mail from my mother's friend. It had some scriptures in it, and when I read it, it mentioned something about God having a plan for me. It talked about the door He has opened for me no man can close. I thought about it for a moment, and then it dawned on me. I haven't received any job offers because they weren't for me. I am slowly but surely beginning to grow spiritually. I just felt so good about it that I had to tell someone."

My heart rejoiced in her delight and that she would even think to share that with me.

When we're living in darkness, God has a way of getting our attention, and that lightbulb moment is wonderful to witness.

One night, about six months later, she called to tell me she was ready to change her life. She wanted to live for God now, and I couldn't wait to hear what had brought her to that point.

"What's going on?" I asked her.

"Before I called you I was sitting here crying in my closet and feeling like I really need to change my priorities. I want to start living my life for God. I try to be the best mother I can be to Tony, and before I quit my last job I had finally received the position I'd worked so hard to achieve. Once I got it, though, Tom told me I always have time for Tony and my job, but not for him."

"Yes, God's been revealing some things to me, as well, about being a wife," I responded.

"I feel so bad, Ken. My focus has been on my career and our finances, but those things aren't as important as my family. Also, when I went to Jamaica a few months ago, I went to church with my mother. At the end of the service my mother wanted me to go up to the front and ask Jesus into my life. She told me to do it for her. I refused. Then a lady took my hand as if to lead me to the front of the church, and I acted like a fool. I pulled away from her and told those people not to touch me. I really acted out. I need to apologize to that church, because I believe God wants me to change some things in my life."

"Well, your desire for Jesus should be about receiving Him, not making your mom happy. I also don't think pulling you to the front of the church was the best approach, but I imagine your mother knew the goodness of a relationship with God and desperately wanted you to know it, too."

I was filled with awe at how God manifests himself. My neighbor asked for direction in beginning a new walk, understanding the Word, and finding a place to worship. I prayed with her and invited

Living in Darkness

her to come to church with me the following Sunday. She agreed, but Sunday morning she overslept. We made plans for the next Sunday, and again, she didn't come.

I imagined Satan's smile of triumph regarding her not stepping one foot into the house of the Lord. I knew she was experiencing spiritual warfare, so I began to pray for her and her husband. However, knowing that God was at work in her life, I could smile too.

God's Word tells us, "In the world ye shall have tribulation: but be of good cheer; I have overcome the world" (John 16:33 KJV). We *will* face temptation and tribulation. There is no *if* about it. There is no running from it, either. The devil is on a mission to recruit both Christians and non-Christians alike.

Imagine going to war without any ammunition or protective gear. How brave do you think you would be? How powerful would you appear to the enemy? What would be your chances of survival? This is essentially a picture of living without Jesus. Satan knows who can defeat him—and it is not us. He yawns at our attempts to fight him in our own strength. Without the Lord, our proper ammunition and gear, we are guaranteed to lose every battle.

Not only is the war taking place around us, but also it is taking place within us—in our minds. Our minds are the war zones in which battles occur daily. We make things easy for Satan when we make no effort to step out of darkness towards Jesus. We give our enemy power and weaken ourselves when we act on the filth he places in our minds. For example, by cursing, gossiping, and lying we speak some of Satan's wicked plans into existence.

Instead of letting the enemy's plans succeed in defeat, we need to use the weapon God has given us: His Word. We should diligently hide the Scriptures in our hearts and meditate on God's Word day and night. When God's Word is hidden in our spiritual hearts, like the blood from our physical hearts, the effects spread throughout our body, soul, and spirit.

As a part of the attacks on our minds, one less noticeable strategy Satan enjoys using is trickery. When we aren't focused on Jesus, Satan can make us believe our actions or intentions are good.

We know that all God created was very good—including you and me—and we were created for His good. His goodness, however, is not found apart from Him and His purpose. His goodness reflects Him—His essence, His power, and His presence. When we are in a place of simply doing good, the urgency to develop a close relationship with the Lord is dead. We foolishly think we don't need Christ that much, leaving some to wonder: What's the big deal about Jesus? However, if Christ is not behind why we do what we do, then either self, something, or someone else is exalted to receive glory.

Some time ago, I spoke with a married woman who did not yet understand the magnitude of her adulterous actions. She'd had an affair with a man at work, and afterwards she considered what happened to be just a physical mistake, giving no thought to the prior months of courting that had led up to the encounter.

She eventually left that job. A few years passed, she received Christ, and she took a job that placed her right back into the work environment with the same man. She chose to interact with this man without considering how she would feel if she were his wife, who was at home and unaware of her own broken marital covenant. She had no intention of confessing to the man's wife, stating she did not want to expose him. Nor did she think she had any personal responsibility to address her.

The woman mentioned a few reasons for her decision to work with and interact with the man again. She said, "Look, Kenyatta, I didn't know the Lord when Joe and I had our affair. Even so, I knew it was wrong at the time, and I told him so. Since then, my husband and I have worked things out. Nothing's going to happen now between Joe and me. Besides, I really need the money this job's going to bring in."

Two points became clear to me as she spoke. First, salvation is the beginning of our walk, which I will discuss in the next chapter. Second, if we believe we have been even a little successful in having a righteous or good walk without Jesus, we set ourselves up for future failure. We forget that even though we have received the Lord, we still need to cleave, or cling, to Him and His way.

With this kind of thinking we tend to misjudge situations, walk back into them, and think that *we* can pull through this time... no problem.

We have probably all experienced thoughts similar to these: *Even before I received Jesus, I didn't do that*; or *I'm not a Christian and I don't even do that*. Satan can have us thinking we can be pretty good without Jesus in our lives, but even Satan knows right from wrong. His or anyone else's choosing to do something right does not make him or that person good. John the Baptist, who told others about the coming of Jesus, did not consider himself good enough to carry Jesus' sandals (Matt. 3:11). Jesus himself said, "No one is good—except God alone" (Mark 10:18).

We glorify ourselves for good behavior when we tell ourselves that at least we *only* did this and did not do that. Our egos are fed, but glory belongs to God. When Jesus is not the reason behind our right actions, we should consider who or what is receiving the glory.

It is only the power of God that can bring every thought into captivity to the obedience of Christ, allowing Jesus to be the center of why we do what we do (2 Cor. 10:5). In our ignorance, Satan uses us for his glory, and often we are unaware of it. Like an enemy at war, Satan is sly with his strategies to attack us. And any time we trust in our own ability, we will be caught off guard.

Our defeating weapon against Satan is Jesus. Having ammunition and gear does not guarantee survival at war, but in the war against Satan, we are guaranteed victory with Jesus Christ as our banner every time.

Time to Reflect

1. What area(s) in your life do you feel a need to change? Explain.

2. Who or what drives most of your major decisions?

3. How do you currently view the purpose of your life?

4. According to the Scriptures, explain how God wants you to live. (Here are a few verses to get you started: Exodus 20:17; Psalm 146:3; Isaiah 43:21; Matthew 4:4; 6:33; 7:24; 28:19–20; Mark 5:19; Romans 10:9; 12:1–2; Ephesians 4:2–3; 5:22–33; James 1:22; 4:7; 5:16.)

Chapter Two

Becoming a Light

I am the way and the truth and the life. No one comes to the Father except through me.

—John 14:6

SALVATION, OR DELIVERANCE from spiritual death, is the only way to begin the process of moving into the light and out of the darkness. Salvation leads to an intimate and permanent relationship with the Lord. God, our Father, loved us so much that He sent His only Son, Jesus Christ, to die for our sins "that whoever believes in him shall not perish but have eternal life" (John 3:16). "Salvation is found in no one else, for there is no other name under heaven given to [us] by which we must be saved" (Acts 4:12). If we believe this we will have eternal life. If we do not believe, we will perish and be eternally separated from God (Mark 16:16).

Jesus is our ladder to God the Father. Salvation assures us access to our Father through Jesus. However, salvation does not guarantee that we will walk in Jesus, who is the light, because we first have to adjust our lives and change the path on which we walk. We become privileged to have a relationship with God as God's redeemed, but we have to exercise our privileges. Without salvation we remain separated from Jesus, and therefore the Father, whether we are aware of it or not.

"If you confess with your mouth, 'Jesus is Lord,' and believe in your heart that God raised Him from the dead, you will be saved. . . . Everyone who calls on the name of the Lord will be saved" (Romans 10:9, 13). This is true regardless of our ethnicity or nationality. Salvation is a result of our faith in Jesus; it is not a birthright. Jesus came into this world to save us from sin and death. He came for sinners, which means He came for you and me. We have been lost in sin since the day we were born. This is a consequence of Adam's sin.

God told Adam not to eat from the tree of knowledge of good and evil, and the bottom line is Adam disobeyed (Genesis 2:17; 3:6). As a result, God sent Adam from His presence (Genesis 3:23). Adam's sin separated him from God and subjected him to death. This consequence was passed on to all people, subjecting us to death, an automatic separation from God, and an inborn sinful nature (Romans 5:12). God's Word tells us that "the wages of sin is death" (Romans 6:23). If we die in sin we are forever banished from God's presence.

The way out of the darkness is only through faith in the Lord Jesus Christ. We are unable to work our way out, so God provides a way by making available His gracious gift to us. The "gift of God is eternal life," and this gift is given by grace (Romans 6:23). God's Word tells us that "by grace are ye saved through faith; and that not of yourselves: it is the gift of God: not of works, lest any man should boast" (Ephesians 2:8–9 KJV). Grace is that unmerited favor given by God.

Since salvation is a gift, it cannot be attained by developing our own intellectual philosophy or by being a good person. Nor can we receive it by "living life to its fullest," doing whatever pleases us. It is a gift that none of us deserve, even if we could earn it. This is the beauty of God's grace.

Consider by whose standards you measure your actions and fullness of life. Your own? Your parents'? Society's? Well, we did not create ourselves. Our parents did not create us (although some parents claim this power and authority). Society did not create us. We were created by *the* Creator, our Father in heaven through Jesus, and He created each of us for His purpose. You are not a mistake. You are special. God's Word talks about "the people I formed for myself that they may proclaim my praise" (Isaiah 43:21). God's grace is extended to bring forth His praise, His glory, and His essence.

We miss His purpose for us when we live in darkness. God desires to use us to manifest His essence—for ourselves, for those we influence, and for those yet to come into our lives. To embark on this journey, the Bible tells us that Jesus is the way, the truth, and the life. No man comes to God the Father but through Jesus (John 14:6). Jesus became our access channel to God because, as I mentioned earlier, at birth we were cut off from God.

During my junior year of college, a fellow student mentioned to me that Jesus was the way to the Father. If I had heard it in church at some point growing up, I hadn't grasped it at all. The incident that led up to our conversation, however, made me more than receptive to the concept.

One evening, Marie (not her real name) came to my dorm room. She told me she sensed something evil in her room and asked to stay in my room for a while. Later, her roommate came down the hall, and Marie left with her. As they entered their room together, Marie passed out. Her roommate grabbed hold of her, yelled for someone to call campus emergency, dragged Marie back across the hall to my room, and placed her in my doorway.

Minutes before this incident, my own roommate had informed me that she sensed evil spirits following her. She tried to convince me that these spirits were trying to get into our room. She went over to the window and forcefully told them to leave.

As we waited for the ambulance to arrive, other students on our floor—curious about all the commotion—gathered at my doorway. My roommate had been labeled a devil worshipper earlier in the semester, so the dorm mother directed her to go to the end of the hall during the incident.

Suddenly, Marie opened her eyes, turned her head towards me, and stared at me in a ghastly and stolid way. To run out of the room meant I had to step over her. Unwilling to risk it, I opened my closet door and moved behind it, barricading myself from her blank gaze. Another student, who'd been studying statistics with me in my room, backed up against the farthest wall, as if hoping the wall would inch backward the harder she leaned. One girl ran to her room and locked herself in when she saw Marie open her eyes.

When the ambulance came and the EMTs went through their procedures, Marie's vital signs checked out normal. Then her chest rose, her back arched stiffly, and she burst out laughing—such a bizarre and evil sound. We all looked at one another with seemingly the same question on our minds. I would guess Marie continued her horrible laughter for an entire minute—eyes closed, head tilted backward, and back arched. For a moment I thought she might be acting, which would have been a relief. But then she opened her eyes and asked what she was doing on the floor. I was sure then that evil was in our midst.

This incident occurred as Hurricane Opal was approaching the Tuskegee University area in Alabama. The entire dorm was mustered in the basement, but several of those who had just watched Marie scrambled for their Bibles prior to heading downstairs for safety.

The hurricane arrived, and the city's emergency alarm continued to sound throughout the town, which added a heightened sense of stress to the situation. We were repeatedly advised to stay indoors, but I took my chances and left the campus.

After everything calmed down the following day, I stood in front of my dorm with some of my friends, discussing Marie's weird behavior. Since the experience was clearly evil, we began to talk about God. One girl asked if I was a Christian. I told her I believed in God, but I did not desire to label myself a Christian or anything else associated with an organized religion.

"Well, do you believe Jesus is the Son of God?"

"Yes," I said.

"You know Jesus is the way to God, right?"

"No."

She looked surprised. "You really didn't know that?"

Her look was so piercing and she seemed so shocked, I wondered whether I should have kept my answer to myself.

That was the end of our conversation, so I said "good-bye" and that was that. However, her reaction and the experience of feeling as if this was something I should have known, like my own name, stayed with me.

I felt odd not knowing about Jesus in that way, but I now know that I was far from being the only one who did not know Jesus is the way to God. If you have only believed in God, but don't have a personal relationship with Him and therefore have not witnessed His presence in your life, perhaps you too need to learn that Jesus is the way to our Father. Moving out of darkness and becoming a light in the world begins with Jesus.

Time to Reflect

1. Some people believe they do not need salvation. Summarize what Romans 2:28–29; 3:9–20; and Galatians 3:22 say about this.

2. Describe your relationship with God.

3. How have you seen your relationship with God mirrored in other relationships in or aspects of your life?

4. If you do not have a relationship with God and would like one, take the time right now to welcome Him into your life. Here is a model prayer you can use:

   Dear heavenly Father,

   I believe Jesus Christ is Your Son. I believe He died and You raised Him from the dead to save me from sin and death. I have sinned, and I ask for Your forgiveness. Please come into my heart and life and direct my paths. Help me to grow into the person You want me to become. Thank You for forgiving and saving me. In Jesus' name, I pray, amen.

Chapter Three

A Whole New You

Do not conform any longer to the pattern of this world, but be transformed by the renewing of your mind.
—Romans 12:2

TO WALK EFFECTIVELY in Jesus Christ, we must be made new in the attitude of our minds and in the condition of our hearts. This requires us to confess our sins in obedience to God. Then we should repent of, or turn away from, the sins that had us bound and turn to God with faith in Jesus. Confession allows us to come spiritually naked before the Lord. It is taking off the mask we wear for others and recognizing the sin behind it.

Unconfessed sin, however, keeps us stagnant and unproductive in the Lord. For this reason we should search our hearts often, asking the Holy Spirit to reveal ways we have displeased the Lord. Keeping ourselves free from sin prepares us to be used by God.

In the past, I longed to be loved and to be in a lifelong, secure relationship. Never wanting to remain in my parents' home, I often imagined that "home sweet home" I hoped would someday come. I poured myself out during my quest to find that home. Yet I found myself heartbroken, filled with unanswered questions.

As time moved on, carrying a broken heart became more common than the feeling of being loved. Soon enough, I became tired of the let downs, the broken promises, the "I don't love you anymore," the "I thought I loved you." I was left to ponder what all of that meant.

Before long I began guarding my heart with a vengeance. I told myself, "No man can do more for me than I can do for myself." I lived by the philosophy "I can live with you or without you." Sure, men were in my life, but they were hardly the committed type. There came a point when I told myself I did not want to expect the commitment, hear the sweet talk, and be let down any longer. Therefore, I began using men in ways I thought I had been used—for pleasure.

I was radically, yet comfortably, indulging in the ways of the world. Yet after searching for love in all the wrong places, and even becoming the mistress in two affairs, a prodding and a struggle began to stir in my spirit. As I looked back over my teenage and young adult life, I wanted to take back the parts of me that I had given away. I was suddenly ashamed of my promiscuity. My connections with some men had been so personally insignificant that I couldn't even remember their names. This disturbed me. And being disturbed led to tears that seemed to flow endlessly—tears of shame, self-pity, and guilt.

Behaviors and attitudes I never thought about came into focus with raw clarity. In time I realized I wanted to change the things I had once justified—both my actions and my thoughts. It was so difficult to look at the path I had traveled that I wanted to lie, even to myself, about where I had been. Even more, I was ashamed to face God, though I was aware that He is omniscient. It was difficult to confess certain sins, especially when I had not had much practice in confessing any sins. As I opened my mouth to confess, nothing came out. This happened again and again until I "purged."

When I finally confessed, a huge burden lifted and my spirit felt sore. I was somehow comforted, believing God had forgiven me. I learned that God looks at our hearts, and as Jonah learned, we cannot hide anything from Him, regardless of how hard we try.

God's Word says, "If we confess our sins, he is faithful and just and will forgive us our sins and purify us from all unrighteousness" (1 John 1:9). This might seem too good to be true. Many people struggle with thinking they've been too bad or have strayed too far. Feelings of unworthiness turn us away from ever believing God would truly accept us as His children. However, Jesus knows the secrets of our hearts, and if your heart is genuine and you truly repent, He can change your heart and make it new. Our Father is a God of compassion. He loves you.

I cannot speak for everyone, but for me, confessing felt like dropping a load of dead weight, and being forgiven made me feel surprisingly special. I felt as if God thought of me as being so important to Him that He accepted me, despite all my flaws. This meant a lot to me, because after becoming totally aware of the road I had taken, I struggled with accepting myself—until I felt God's embrace.

Something happened as I moved on with my life, though. God's Word was not hidden in my heart, and when I went back into the world, I was still flailing about, trying to find my way. There was no repentance. Although I had accepted Jesus into my heart as a little girl, His Word was not in me and I hadn't learned the principle of allowing Him to be Lord of my life. With the lack of grounding in His Word, I was unable to turn away from sin and move toward God. Little did I know (though He knew) that I was on a journey that would lead to Him. God has an awesome way of showing His glory through our sins.

Never acknowledging how our behaviors are viewed in the eyes of the Lord will keep us in darkness. After acknowledging our sins and confessing them, we ought to experience behavioral and psychological changes due to repentance. Our goal should be to act and think like Jesus. It is not enough to internally decide to stop sinning and then continue to walk along the same path that tempts us. We have to feed our minds righteous food to have a virtuous walk and often have to change some of our ways.

> When tempted, no one should say, "God is tempting me." For God cannot be tempted by evil, nor does he tempt anyone; but each one is tempted when, by his own evil desire, he is dragged away and enticed. Then, after desire has conceived, it gives birth to sin; and sin, when it is full-grown, gives birth to death.
> —James 1:13–15

For example, if you have been tempted and have given yourself over to lust, which led you to such things as fornication, promiscuity, infidelity, pornography, or other immoral acts, you might need to change a few things for repentance to be evident. You may find it worthwhile to change your environment, the people you most often socialize with, the movies you watch, the books you read, the music you listen to, the places you go, or anything else that would in any way promote or give access to the temptation that has lured you to sin.

Repentance should be an observable walk away from our sins towards God. Keep in mind, however, that we cannot walk towards God on our own. God enables us and gives us access to come to Him. Our minds have to be fueled with the Word of God, and it has to be stored in our hearts in order for us to be able to walk in one accord with God. Otherwise, we will eventually fall again into the same temptation or become entrapped in some other kind of sin, because we will be the same old spiritually weak people. Since there is no sin, but holiness, around God, it is only through our closeness to God that we experience a true turning away from our sins (Psalm 93:5).

If we are to walk worthy of our Father in Christ, we must be transformed by the renewing of our minds (Romans 12:2). This is not a one-time decision. Each day, with everything we do, we are to look through the eyes of the Lord and offer ourselves as living sacrifices to Him (Romans 12:1). We can see through the eyes of the Lord when we spend time in His Word and receive revelation through the Holy Spirit.

Have you tried to change for the better by doing what you think is right? Righteousness is not just right behavior. Likewise, the essence of holiness in a person is not measured by the number of times he or she does right behavior. Our ways are neither holy nor righteous if obeying and honoring the Lord is not our motivation. Righteousness is the result of our obedience to God, despite the way we see things (Deuteronomy 6:25). Holiness is the result of becoming slaves to God (Romans 6:22). The renewing of our minds and process of creating a new spirit within us begins with the Lord.

As long as we do our part and offer ourselves to God and His will, God will do His part and allow the Holy Spirit to transform us. "The sinful nature desires what is contrary to the Spirit, and the Spirit what is contrary to the sinful nature" (Galatians 5:17). If we live by the Spirit we will not gratify the desires of our sinful nature (Galatians 5:16).

Time to Reflect

1. Identify sin you have not confessed to the Lord. Confess it to God in prayer.

2. Has a lack of confession affected your relationship with the Lord? If so, how?

3. According to Galatians 5:19, what are some acts of the sinful nature?

4. According to Galatians 5:22–23, when we are made over as new people, what virtues are manifested in us through the Holy Spirit?

Chapter Four

Talking to God

> *And without faith it is impossible to please God, because anyone who comes to him must believe that he exists and that he rewards those who earnestly seek him.*
> —Hebrews 11:6

ONCE WE BELIEVE through faith and receive Jesus into our lives, God's Word encourages us to fellowship with Him in prayer. We are encouraged to pray to the Father in Jesus' name, as Jesus' authorized representatives. According to His will, whatever we ask in His name He will do it (John 14:13–14). The power of prayer is not found in our words, but in our faith in the power of Jesus and in our trusting that His will is no mistake.

Praying is often thought of as talking to God. However, everyone does not have the privilege of being heard in prayer (John 9:31). Although prayer is viewed as talking to God, our talking should not be mere words. When we talk to God, whether with memorized Scripture or not, whether alone or with others, the words from our mouths should be poured from our hearts. The length of our prayers does not matter. God delights in our sincerity when we come to Him.

Sometimes we may experience unanswered prayers. When this happens, consider looking at what is happening on the inside instead of focusing on what is happening on the outside. This may seem simple, but for some, like me, this isn't as easy as it sounds.

We cannot confess what we do not recognize. We tend to justify, excuse, and deny our actions because it comforts and protects us. By nature we are very selfish beings. This hinders us from being transparent before the Lord, and when we come to the Lord wearing the same mask that we present to the world, we cannot grow spiritually. We cannot hide anything from God, but we do have the ability to hide things from others and even ourselves. When we have hidden junk in our hearts, it's pretty difficult to walk in agreement with the Lord.

I certainly don't claim to know all of the answers pertaining to unanswered prayer. Still, there are a few areas I explored with God when I experienced unanswered prayer. Boy, was I enlightened. Here are a few reasons our prayers may go unanswered:

- **Praying with selfish motives.** God's Word teaches us to "Do nothing out of selfish ambition or vain conceit, but in humility consider others better than" ourselves (Philippians 2:3). The Lord knows our hearts (Acts 1:24). Even when we think our hearts are clean, He can see the junk that rests in hidden compartments.

- **Praying not according to the will of God.** Jesus said, "For I have come down from heaven not to do my will but to do the will of him who sent me" (John 6:38). Jesus' purpose is to do the will of God. He is not about to change courses and jump onto our boat. We have to jump onto His boat. Jesus knew the will of God because He communed with His Father intimately (Mark 14:36). Like Jesus, we also learn of God's will as we spend time seeking Him and communing with Him.

- **Praying with an unforgiving heart.** Mark 11:25 states, "When you stand praying, if you hold anything against anyone, forgive him, so that your Father in heaven may forgive you your sins." Unforgiveness is a gateway to self-righteousness and self-fulfillment. It holds impurities in our hearts and blocks us from living in one accord with the Lord. God has bestowed His mercy on us. Likewise, we are to display this same kind of mercy from our hearts and forgive those who have offended us.

- **Praying without faith.** God's Word teaches, "Whatever you ask for in prayer, believe that you have received it, and it will be yours" (Mark 11:24). It is not enough to believe Jesus exists. We must believe in His authority, His Word, and His faithfulness. Jesus healed many according to their faith. "Without faith it is impossible to please God" (Hebrews 11:6).

- **Not praying in the name of Jesus.** Only Jesus has the authority. God's Word assures us, "Whatsoever ye shall ask in my name, that will I do, that the Father may be glorified in the Son. If ye shall ask any thing in my name, I will do it" (John 14:13–14 KJV). No one comes to the Father but through Jesus (John 14:6). Once Jesus dwells in us, we are extended the privilege of praying in His name. We were separated from God because of our sin, and Jesus is our only link.

- **Praying without praise.** "The people have I formed for myself; they shall show forth my praise" (Isaiah 43:21 KJV). God is sovereign in all of heaven and earth (Matthew 11:25). There is none greater (1 Chronicles 16:25). How gracious is He (1 Peter 2:3 KJV). How fitting it is to praise Him at all times (2 Chronicles 30:21). God inhabits the praise of those who belong to Him (Psalm 22:3 KJV). It seems to please Him to see His children revere Him in this manner.

- **Praying and then giving up.** God's Word teaches us to "pray continually" (1 Thessalonians 5:17). He demonstrates how He favors persistence in prayer in Luke 18:1–8, the parable of the persistent widow.

> In a certain town there was a judge who neither feared God nor cared about men. And there was a widow in that town who kept coming to him with the plea, "Grant me justice against my adversary." For some time he refused. But finally he said to himself, "Even though I don't fear God or care about men, yet because this widow keeps bothering me, I will see that she gets justice, so that she won't eventually wear me out with her coming!"
>
> —Luke 18:2-5

How much more will God listen to us if we persist! "He rewards those who earnestly seek him" (Hebrews 11:6).

- **Praying without confessing and repenting.** Confessing and repenting go hand in hand. God's Word says, "Confess your sins to each other and pray for each other so that you may be healed. The prayer of a righteous man is powerful and effective" (James 5:16). The Israelites, God's chosen people, were guilty of unrighteousness. God called them to repentance in Ezekiel 18:30 (and many other places in the Bible), and likewise, He has called us to turn away from our sins and become new.

- **Praying without a fear of the Lord.** "The fear of the Lord is the beginning of wisdom" (Proverbs 9:10). This kind of fear is reverential, regarding Jesus' sovereignty in heaven and on earth. "Through the fear of the Lord a man avoids evil" (Proverbs 16:6).

We have to lose ourselves if we desire to be used as the Lord's instruments. I struggle with this most when I have been hurt. I have had to ask the Lord, "Is there anything in my heart that is not of You? If so, please reveal to me what needs to be changed." I find that although I may want to please God, my feelings can cloud my mind, and my intentions go astray. Sometimes we sin knowingly and intentionally, while other times we are not even aware when we have offended our Savior. It is appropriate to ask the Lord to bring to light those hidden sins and to prepare us to receive His answer (1 Corinthians 4:5). He wants us to rely on Him to get to know who we are. After all, He knows us better than we know ourselves.

As we move into a relationship with God, we should be careful not to get into a habit of praying and then immediately resuming our daily business. Spend some time in silence, acknowledging God's presence by listening. Welcome and listen to the Holy Spirit, who dwells inside you. In your silence allow the Lord to reveal any changes that need to be made. Allow Him to reveal His plan for you.

Receiving revelations from God could be the beginning of some level of spiritual growth and wisdom. It is not unusual for some of these insights to bring forth a cascade of tears. Those tears may be an indication of a broken and willing heart. Welcome them, and thank God for speaking to you.

When spending time with the Lord, don't try to duplicate the experiences of others. Their relationship with God will be different than yours. Focus on communing and fellowshipping with Jesus with your whole heart. The rest is up to God.

At times we may feel as though God is absent. Although we know He is omnipresent, we may not feel His presence. During these still times, I think it's best to wait. I wait on making life decisions and instead retreat into His Word, as if to say, "I know You have a purpose for me, even in this silence."

God desires for us to be bold enough to trust Him and to remain faithful, always remembering His omnipotence, His faithfulness, and His Word. He can give us more than we could ever think of asking for (Eph. 3:20–21). God reminds us in His Word to "ask and it shall be given you; seek and ye shall find; knock, and it shall be opened unto you" (Matthew 7:7–8 KJV). Notice that each action stated—*ask, seek,* and *knock*—has a result: *given, find,* and *opened.* God promises results once we act in faith.

Time to Reflect

1. What can you conclude about your prayer life?

2. Identify any recognized hindrances in your prayer life.

3. How can you improve your fellowship with the Lord in prayer?

Chapter Five

Trials and Tribulations

Consider it pure joy, my brothers, whenever you face trials of many kinds, because you know that the testing of your faith develops perseverance. Perseverance must finish its work so that you may be mature and complete, not lacking anything.
—James 1:2–4

TRIALS AND TRIBULATIONS are the tests or means by which we grow. God's Word tells us these times are necessary for our maturity and completeness. Through them we grow in our faith, grow bolder in the Lord, and grow in our intimacy with the Lord. Our trials and tribulations ultimately become both our opportunities for personal growth through perseverance and our opportunities to see God's power at work.

Scripture tells us to consider it joy whenever we face trials of many kinds (James 1:2). I do not believe this means that we cannot come before God in vulnerability and honestly express ourselves to Him in the midst of some devastating event. He created us with emotions, and we might experience anger, distress, fear, or other emotions in any given circumstance. At the same time, when we face our trials God wants us to trust in Him with all our hearts and not lean on our own understanding. In all our ways we must acknowledge Him, and He will direct our paths (Proverbs 3:5–6, paraphrase). God wants us to believe that whatever we face, we can get through it with Him. And because He is present with us, He wants us to go through our trials, not just sneak around them or turn away from them.

As a teenager, I experienced a paralyzing sense of devastation after someone crossed boundaries by making sexual advances toward me. The trust between us was broken, and I felt shattered to the core of my being. The whole thing became indescribably surreal after I gathered enough courage to tell, following a particular incident, and the violation was treated as if I had never mentioned a word about it. The humiliation was more than I thought I could carry. All I could think about was running away. Several times I stood by my bedroom window, tearfully wondering where I could go and how I would support myself. I questioned the sincerity of love for me. Many years later, an unusual statement was made and I saw for the first time that instead of being seen as just a child, I had also been seen and treated as a threat. Nonetheless, I felt betrayed and misunderstood. As a result, I was driven to gain independence, and my education became my security to achieve it.

I was filled with a traumatizing fear from the betrayal, but at some point, everything left my consciousness. I buried the memories completely. While I was a senior in college, I started dreaming about my past. I experienced what I thought were nightmares for the first time in my life. Every night for approximately a week, I would awake in a panic, thinking everything I dreamed felt so real. Once I woke up, however, I couldn't finish the scenario I had dreamed about. The experience resembled a crack in an iceberg. After chipping away at some of the details for several nights, the cracks spread, and more details were revealed to me while I was awake. Though I was a psychology major, even listening to a lecture on molestation didn't trigger anything in my subconscious.

"How could I just forget everything?" I've often wondered. Perhaps I was just unaware of the totality of what sexual abuse encompassed. At the time, I was aware of the sexual penetration part, which did not describe my tribulations, but later I learned there were other aspects. Sexual abuse can be physical, emotional, overt (sexual stimulation by means of voyeurism and exhibitionism), covert (inappropriate sexual talking and questioning), or a boundary violation. When the nature of the sexual act is developmentally inappropriate for at least one of the participants, it is sexual abuse. When the balance of power and authority between the individuals is unequal, as in parent to child or supervisor to subordinate, it is sexual abuse.

After putting together the pieces of my dreams, my old childhood feelings flooded my body again. Ironically, this occurred at a time in my life when I had been guaranteed a job as an Air Force officer, so I would be leaving the old and moving into the new. Overcoming the effects of sexual abuse was a trial I was willing to face. However, the power this had over me was overwhelming.

Years later, I turned to the Lord. When I did, I saw that God allowed me to have these revelations when I did because He knew exactly what I was capable of bearing at that time. He knew what would later become of me and exactly what He had planned for me as a result.

What did or will become of me is still in the making, but I am glad to be able to say that God has shown me so much of Himself through trials. The Lord is my refuge and my fortress, and it is in Him that I have received my strength to cope with the effects—the bottled up anger and the quiet rage—these experiences have caused. I have relied on Jesus for wisdom on how to move forward in love and to move on from my past. I have been stretched spiritually and freed through forgiveness from the binding effects of sin.

Forgiveness is not saying that we now condone what someone has done or that we forget, but that we no longer hold it against them. Forgiveness is releasing the attitude that someone owes us something. It is no longer allowing that "wrong" to hinder us from caring for and expressing love toward another. Forgiveness releases the person from the justice he or she might deserve and invites a spirit of mercy and love, *despite* what is deserved.

Satan is working hard to win us over, and our intellectual willpower is not enough to keep us standing firm during our trials and tribulations. If you have not already experienced it, you will find that willpower fluctuates, just as our feelings do. We are all very vulnerable to the enemy when we are not pressing toward Jesus. God's Word states that "the heart is deceitful above all things, and desperately wicked: who can know it?" (Jeremiah 17:9 KJV). If God's Word says this about us, how can we trust our own ways and walk through our trials with assurance that we will overcome them?

The truth is that we cannot trust our own ways. God, however, is forever faithful and unwavering (1 Corinthians 1:9). It is only with Him that we can walk *through* our trials and come out shining on the other side. Our relationship with the Lord will certainly be reflected in each step. At times it may feel like it, but we are not alone in our experiences. When we submit ourselves to Him, God's glory can shine through all situations.

Time to Reflect

1. Describe a trial in your life in which you felt as if you were unable to go *through* it and as a result walked around or away from it.

2. List the names of those whom you have not forgiven and why.

3. Ask God to give you the willingness and the strength—through Him—to forgive those who have hurt you.

    Dear heavenly Father,

Your are all powerful and You are a God of miracles. I have kept an unforgiving heart toward _____ [name(s) of person or people] and I have allowed it to keep me from growing in Your Spirit. Please forgive me. Allow Your ways to become my ways. Help me to serve and please You each day. Show me how to bless, even my offender. I cannot do this without You. I come to You in the name of Jesus, with a heart willing to serve. Give me the strength not to be conformed to this world, but to be transformed by the renewing of my mind. Please make me over. Cleanse my heart of all the bitterness, shame, anger, judgment, fear, and pain. Fill me with Your love, patience, forgiveness, and humility in its stead. Touch my mind, Lord, and help me to focus on whatever is true, honest, just, pure, lovely, and of good report. Amen.

Chapter Six

Surrendering

All things work together for good to them that love God, to them who are the called according to his purpose.
—Romans 8:28 KJV

GOD IS IN control.
We all have a tendency at times to do things our own way. My way has taken me down dead-end streets and brought me to crossroads where I didn't know which way to go. Sometimes I got tired of my way, although I would still act as if everything was under control. When we live our lives as if we are in control, eventually we get a little tired of the mess it creates.

"Offer your bodies as living sacrifices, holy and pleasing to God—this is your spiritual act of worship" (Romans 12:1). God desires for each of us to worship Him by surrendering our ways. Surrendering is evidence that our eyes are on heavenly purposes. It is an act of faith. It is a sacrifice that expresses to God that we belong to Him. Surrendering expresses that we know His ways are better than our ways and we are releasing our ways in exchange for His. Surrendering is an absolute way to get out of the holes we dig on our own.

Some people search endlessly to find or create meaning in their lives. Have you ever heard people mention that they "plan to live life to the fullest"? That "this is what life is all about"? I could be wrong, but I've never taken this to mean that they planned on living life to the fullest in Christ. Rather, they wanted to pursue personal endeavors and explore areas that did not include Christ. If we are not careful, we can set ourselves up to strive after personal pleasures that are outside of God's will. Then, after we achieve our goals and after we've tried all sorts of things at least once, we boast, believing we are experiencing "what life is all about."

Why were we created? We were created to glorify God and for His pleasure. If we desire to live a life filled with meaning and purpose, we have to seek God's will for our lives. The more we become available to God and surrender to doing what the Lord created us to do, the more we will see Him at work in our lives. The more we are obedient to His will and join God in His plan, the more we will live out the true purpose of our lives.

When I began my walk with Jesus and began to grow spiritually, God gave me a quiet revelation about the fondness I had for going to church and being with the people there. He showed me that many church people appear to have surrendered to Him, but in fact, their words do not necessarily reflect what is in their hearts. God revealed this to me at a time when my trust in the church and its members was increasing greatly. When He opened my eyes, I saw that some people were going to church often enough to serve in the church, but they disregarded the concept of *being* God's church, while others were caught in the cycle of tradition and idolatry. Only God can see the contents of a person's heart, but these contents spill over into our attitudes and actions. Through this revelation, God showed me that surrendering begins with the heart.

True surrender to our Father gives us an eternal perspective, because it is not about us and the here and now that we tend to get entangled in. When Jesus reveals Himself to us, He does not want us to withhold the good news about Him from others. We are to go and teach others to obey everything Jesus has commanded (Matthew 28:19–20). We must raise our eyes above the here and now and focus on building up the kingdom of God.

When we continue to surrender to God each day, we continue to grow more and more. Like a baby learns from a parent, we begin to learn the truth about Jesus, the embodied Word of God. As we grow, we learn more. As we realize that our childhood knowledge was incomplete, we begin to test and apply more and more truth to our lives. We then mature and begin to teach others what we now know through experience is truth. At the end of this process, we end up resembling the parent who taught us truth.

Regardless of how we got into the hole of following our own way, we are accountable for our actions. Whether our parents were loving and good or abusive and neglectful, we have a perfect parent in God the Father. We will begin to resemble Him the same way some grow to resemble their earthly parents who taught them.

Surrendering requires us to trust that the Lord will do what He says He will do. No matter what a situation looks like to us, God has a bigger plan. His Word reminds us that "in all things God works for the good of those who love him" (Romans 8:28). Although we cannot see the end, God already knows it. And it is good. However, if we turn away from God, we will find ourselves stuck in the holes we have created.

Have you ever experienced something that caused worry, and the worry then caused physiological changes, such as tiredness, loss of appetite, headaches, or even ulcers? Worrying is a means to keep us in bondage, and the more we worry, the stronger the grip of that bondage becomes.

In Matthew 6:34, Jesus teaches us not to worry about tomorrow because He will provide. Rather than worrying, we are to spend our time seeking God and His righteousness before everything else (Matthew 6:33). When we sincerely offer ourselves and our daily situations to God in faith, God not only hears us calling on Him, but He is also ready to help. When we surrender, God meets us right where we are.

I recall facing some difficulties as a new stepparent. (This was my first experience in parenting.) My son felt he had to choose between his mother and father after their divorce. So he took on the responsibility of trying to please his mother, and part of this meant rejecting me when he was either with his mother or when he spoke with her on the phone.

Needless to say, I was hurt. I adored children, but I started to feel as if I had to guard my heart from this child. I believed this was a safe way to deal with the situation, but it wasn't what my heart desired. Soon I became irritable and depressed. I was unmotivated to get out of bed, shower, eat, or help feed the children. I was overwhelmed with the drama that came along with becoming a stepparent. I had an urge to run away from it all.

When my son came home in the summers from his home with his mother, I saw negative changes in him, due to the wounded and hardened hearts that existed in both of his homes. This rested heavily on my heart. He seemed emotionally confused and trapped—unable to openly receive and give the love that existed in the only homes he knew for fear of hurting someone's feelings. He appeared to be living a double life, yet he was so young. The pressure. The sadness. The secrecy of his feelings. I wondered what kind of man he would become. I thought about my husband, Dan, who experienced the same struggle of siding with one of his parents after their divorce and ostracizing the other. I saw how this impacted him for the worse and how, in what seemed to be a generational cycle, it was impacting our son in a similar fashion. I was saddened as I observed all of this, but I didn't know what to do.

Nothing I did seem to help. I thought, "This can't be the way it's supposed to be." Soon, I lost hope, thinking of all the wrong I'd done digging the hole I was in and wondering, "Maybe this *is* the way it's supposed to be for *me*." I felt lost. Although I didn't have a relationship with God, I went running to Him for help—like many of us do when we need help, even when we do not have a relationship with God. I literally begged for God's help on the bathroom floor knowing the dismal choices I had envisioned. What other good choices did I have?

One morning, after crying out to the Lord on that bathroom floor earlier in the week, I woke up and sat on the side of my bed. I felt as if someone had literally pulled me up and placed me in this position. As I sat staring at a plain white wall, it was as if someone whispered a command: "Love." I suddenly realized that children are from God and they belong to Him. Then I understood that this son of mine was God's child, and I needed to love him boldly, not secretly. There was no need to guard my heart, because if I exemplified *God's* love, *He* would be pleased with me. (Reflecting God's love toward others is a key principle that God teaches in His Word, but during those days I would not have had a clue about where to look for it in Scripture.)

I stood up in amazement, wondering where that message had come from. I knew it hadn't come from me, so I quickly embraced the fact that the Lord was speaking to me. He was calling *me*. A sense of awe blanketed my awareness. I began to believe that despite the odds, God had a real purpose for me in parenting, and God had a real purpose for my son in my life. Although I knew the journey wouldn't be easy, I was somehow comforted by knowing exactly what I was supposed to do in my circumstances. From that experience, God gave me a strong and conscious desire to really know Him and learn how to live my life for Him.

As the Lord revealed things, I surrendered, and over the next few years, I began to see wonderful changes in our family dynamics. There are still trials, but the attitude in my heart changed. God turned my dislike for stepparenting into a way to honor Him. It has truly been a blessing in disguise.

Jesus was in the midst of it all. He showed me that my purpose was not just for me, but also for my family, which He would later increase, and for those who would later come into my life. I just needed to surrender and follow God's direction.

Time to Reflect

1. In what areas of your life do you find yourself doing things your way?

2. What have been the results?

3. How do you feel about the results? Is God pleased?

4. Describe what you think surrendering to God's way in these areas would look like.

5. Take time right now to pray about these areas. If you're not yet willing to surrender to His way, ask Him to give you a willing heart. Write down your petitions, and continue to pray for these areas.

Chapter Seven

Knowing God's Word

The natural man receiveth not the things of the Spirit of God: for they are foolishness unto him: neither can he know them, because they are spiritually discerned.
—1 Corinthians 2:14 KJV

GOD'S WORD, THE Bible, is the ultimate source of authority for our lives. Directions for handling anything we encounter can be found in His Word. We cannot grow in Christ without knowing God's Word and understanding it through the Holy Spirit. This goes beyond simply hearing it in church; it includes reading, studying, memorizing, and meditating on the Word of God on our own, as well as spending time in prayer.

Although I still have much more to learn, there was a time when understanding anything in the Bible was difficult for me. Prior to becoming a disciple of Christ, I remember attending a local church with Dan. Many times I left without understanding most or any of the pastor's sermons, which were heavily laced with Scripture. I felt as if the pastor was talking way over my head, and Dan had to explain the referenced stories from the Bible to me. I resolved that attending church just was not enough for me to progress in knowing God's Word. I needed to *study* it.

When I began reading God's Word, I did not have a clear understanding of God's big picture. I was lost. Since I could not understand God's Word on my own, I asked Him for understanding. Wow, what a difference! Sometimes I am still amazed that these are the same words I read years ago. God's Word teaches us that "the natural man receiveth not the things of the Spirit of God: for they are foolishness unto him: neither can he know them, because they are spiritually discerned" (1 Corinthians 2:14 KJV). What started as something foreign to me became food for my spirit.

Second Timothy 2:15 says, "Study to show thyself approved unto God" (KJV). Studying God's Word daily edifies our spirits and builds our relationship with the Lord. Each of us can discover growth in our spirits through studying God's Word each day. We can worship God by making studying His Word and doing what it says a way of life. Some of us want changes to occur in our lives, but we are unwilling to change how we live in order for those changes to occur. It is not wise to base our approach on mere willpower, because willpower comes and goes. Studying God's Word is our source for spiritual maturity. It is our daily bread.

"In the beginning was the Word, and the Word was with God, and the Word was God" (John 1:1). Spending time with God requires us to spend time with Jesus through His Word. God's Word, embodied in Jesus, has the power to change our hearts (Luke 4:32). All that we need in this world is in His Word. By diligently studying God's Word, we show our total dependence on Him to live our lives righteously. By believing and acting according to His Word, we express our faith. We acknowledge that without Him we are lost; we are weak. God is pleased with our desire to know Him and to grow in Him. As we seek Him, He will come near to us (James 4:8). And during this personal time in the presence of the Lord, we will discover God's will for our lives.

In addition to studying the Word, it is important to memorize it. Memorizing Scripture is a means of hiding God's Word in our hearts to help us not to sin (Psalm 119:11). It protects us from being fooled by the lies of Satan. When God's Word is in us, we have easy access to it to meditate on it and to pray His Word in the midst of temptation. I cannot think of anything more true, honest, just, pure, lovely, of good report, virtuous, or praiseworthy to meditate on (see Phil. 4:8).

We've all had to study and memorize information for a test. This memorization process requires us to become focused on whatever information we are trying to retain. When we finally memorize the information, we can take the test with confidence. We can produce right answers. We can pass the test.

When we memorize God's Word, we are easily reminded of what God thinks about everyday situations we encounter. Memorizing Scripture prepares us for tests in the world. When we are prepared through God's Word, we can stand with confidence, produce righteous responses, and pass our life tests.

In this world, it is much too easy to get sidetracked and waste our time listening to music that promotes sexuality, drugs, crime, and hatred. We, particularly women, feel as if we have to answer the phone each time it rings and take part in the gossip others bring to us. We maintain a ritual of watching sitcoms and the news. We're often so busy that we forget to invite the Lord to join us in our daily walk.

Monitoring what we feed our minds is crucial. Some things feed our flesh, some feed our minds, and some feed our spirits. Just going with the flow and leaving to chance what society will feed us next will guarantee failure at our life tests.

Here are a few suggestions for taking control over what goes into your mind:

- The next time you get into your car, listen to music that praises the Lord and promotes His love. There is just something in the spirit of Christ-centered music that can prompt our hearts to enter into a higher level of praise.

- Consider using your "drive time" as an opportunity to meditate on God's Word, listen to spiritually edifying books on CD, and pray (with your eyes open, of course!).

- Watch less television, especially if you have children. Instead, rent or borrow movies from the library that are praiseworthy or will sow good seeds of righteousness for you and your family.

As I sought a deeper relationship with the Lord, I learned through a Bible study class the importance of meditation. (By no means am I referring to new age meditation here.) I am referring to an act of devotion by consecrating our minds and consciously setting aside life issues, while intentionally focusing on God's Word as it applies to us. Since then, meditation has been an essential part of my spiritual growth. However, at the time, the concept of meditation was new to me, and simply hearing about it didn't entice me enough to try it. As I envisioned myself reading, studying, and meditating on God's Word *that* intensely and regularly, I felt a bit intimidated. I thought that if I needed to meditate as part of growing in my relationship with the Lord, then I would not be doing much growing. I was a mother of twin, preschool-age boys and a baby daughter, and I spent my time being their teacher and playmate. I wore the remains of spit-up and other spills until they went to bed. I had a household to maintain and a marriage to nurture. I was just too busy to meditate.

Surprisingly, these feelings subsided when I actually began praying, reading, and studying God's Word as a part of a Bible study workbook. For the first time, reading God's Word was not just like reading another book. *These* words ignited my spirit. They became *alive*, and I experienced a plethora of feelings due to the Holy Spirit's conviction within me. I was enlightened, and I desired more. Naturally, it seemed, I found myself meditating on God's Word.

Meditation is simply a deeper personal focus on God's Word. Since our walk with Christ is personal, it provides a channel for us to personally experience God's revelation through the Holy Spirit. Its practice is essential.

Time to Reflect

1. Describe your current commitment to spending time with God and studying His Word. What, if anything, would you like to change?

2. What part of the day works best for you to study God's Word? Establish the best time for you to study His Word daily for at least ten to fifteen minutes and commit to it.

3. Following are a few Scripture verses to get you started in meditating and memorizing. You may want to choose one for the entire week, or focus on a different one each day.

Psalm 119:11	Romans 6:23	Galatians 5:22–23
Psalm 146:2	Romans 8:28	Ephesians 2:8–10
Matthew 7:7–8	Romans 10:9	Philippians 1:6
Matthew 28:18–20	Romans 12:1–2	Philippians 4:6
Mark 16:15–16	1 Corinthians 2:14	Philippians 4:8
John 3:16	1 Corinthians 10:13	2 Timothy 3:16
John 14:13–14	2 Corinthians 5:17	2 Peter 1:20–21
Romans 1:16	2 Corinthians 9:7	
Romans 3:23	Galatians 5:16	

Chapter Eight

Hearing God's Voice

He will guide you into all truth. He will not speak on his own; he will speak only what he hears.
—John 16:13

SOME OF US get a little discouraged when we hear others say, "God told me . . ." We compare ourselves and either wonder how can we tell if God is talking to us or if those people were telling the truth about God talking to them. God revealed to me that the more I searched God's Word and asked Him for wisdom and understanding, the more I experienced the Word of God, or the more He manifested Himself in my life.

Jesus told His disciples He would send a Counselor when He left, who is the Holy Spirit. He said, "The Holy Spirit, whom the Father will send in my name, will teach you all things and will remind you of everything I have said to you" (John 14:26). The Holy Spirit speaks from within us, since that is where He dwells once we receive Jesus as our Savior. It is the Holy Spirit who *convicts* our hearts. As we spend time in the Word, the Holy Spirit *reveals* truth to us regarding our spiritual wisdom and understanding. Jesus explained that the Holy Spirit will bring glory to Him by taking from what is His and making it known to us (John 16:14). When we find ourselves praying and searching for answers, the Holy Spirit *leads* us to specific answers to our prayers. Other times, the Holy Spirit *reminds* us of God's Word that we might be obedient and please God.

As I spent time in God's Word, suddenly I was not this mature, beautiful lady any longer, spiritually speaking. I noticed that I was really quite ugly and selfish. I realized what a baby I was spiritually. I fell short in so many areas. Although I felt I was somewhat knowledgeable, many times I acted on something and did not know what I was doing. I made many decisions based on what I wanted and was influenced by the world, not by Jesus. I recognized my unwillingness to quickly and unquestioningly do God's will. To change my ways, I had to sacrifice and come out of my comfort zone. I realized that this walk with Jesus was not going to be an easy one.

The Holy Spirit allows us to hear God's voice through the Word of God. Initially, His manifestation is similar to noticing anything else we may notice for the first time. For example, a new sound or noise may barely gain our attention at first. We may not know or even care where it came from. However, the more we hear it or spend time around it, the more attention we give to listening to what it actually is.

Similarly, the more attention we give to listening to the Holy Spirit within us, the more we will learn what God's voice sounds like. The "attention" I'm speaking of is our time spent in the Word. When we immerse ourselves in God's Word, we will discover God's voice and get to know Him better. Our relationship with the Lord is personal, which means we should take the time to read what He actually said rather than relying only on what others say about the Word. As God fills our hearts with His essence, we will see Him manifest Himself in our lives.

Some time ago, a man, who didn't know the Lord, told me he was preparing to go through a divorce. I shared with him that things could change in his marriage if he started with himself. I told him he could win his wife over, and possibly motivate her to change her life as well, if he would first start to live for Christ. To my surprise, he asked me what if God was *telling* him to get a divorce, yet he hadn't tried Jesus. He believed his life would be better if he divorced his wife, because in his mind, she was the one with the problems, not him (though he did acknowledge that he was not perfect).

When we're faced with a decision, we may think we've heard the answer, but to discern and know whether or not what we've heard is of God, we need to know His Word. The Holy Spirit may manifest Himself differently in each of our lives, but we can be sure of this one thing: He absolutely will not go against the Word of God. His counsel will always be consistent with the Word. Jesus said, "He will guide you into all truth. He will not speak on his own; he will speak only what he hears" (John 16:13). When the voices we hear contradict God's Word, we can know they are not of God, but of the enemy.

Time to Reflect

1. Consider what you know about the Word of God. How have you attained the majority of that knowledge?

2. What specific things can you do to increase your ability to know when God is talking to you?

3. Make a commitment to read, study, and meditate on God's Word and pray for at least fifteen minutes each day for forty days. If you would rather be directed on where to begin, using a Bible study workbook might be helpful. During this period, keep track of your commitment by journaling your appointments with God, along with prayer requests, revelations, feelings, and answers to prayer.

Chapter Nine

The War

We wrestle not against flesh and blood, but against principalities, against powers, against the rulers of the darkness of this world, against spiritual wickedness in high places.
—Ephesians 6:12 KJV

THE BIBLE WARNS us of the war into which we were born. This war is spiritual, and it has two sides: Satan and his forces are fighting against God. As ambassadors of Christ, we are a threat to the enemy. Therefore, Satan attacks with all kinds of evil tactics, hoping to turn us from the will of God.

When Satan attacks, he often attacks our minds. What he injects into our minds contaminates our spirits. He unloads feelings of resentment, pride, revenge, guilt, shame, self-righteousness, doubt, hopelessness, fear, depression, and more that hinder our spiritual growth. When we accept and believe what Satan puts in our minds, he can drive us to desperate measures, because we start trying to find someone or something to rescue us. This is why people turn to drugs, alcohol, adultery, and even suicide.

This reminds me of a woman I knew who was experiencing a very difficult period in her life. She expressed feelings of worry, fear, depression, helplessness, and hopelessness. After umpteen hours of exhausting telephone support, believing everything could work out for her good if she would put her eyes on the Lord, I suggested that she talk to God about what He wanted her to receive from her experience. I believed her hardship was happening for a much bigger reason than she thought. Sadly, she couldn't see beyond her circumstances, and she told me she wanted someone "real" to turn to besides God—someone who would talk back to her. My heart sank because I knew she didn't really understand the depth of God's love and care for her. Ultimately, I prayed for her spiritual growth.

This woman didn't understand that there is no one more real than God, our Father. There is no one more consistent, no one more righteous, and no one mightier. Yet people cannot claim or understand this without faith. It is during those very difficult times when the fragility or strength in our relationship with God shows most. And regardless of the strength of our relationship with God, Satan tries endlessly to undermine that relationship and to convince us that God doesn't really care about us.

I believed the devil was real before I asked Jesus to be Lord of my life. However, without a relationship with the Lord (the only place from which I could gain true wisdom), I was blinded to just how real Satan's existence is in this world and in my life. I did not acknowledge his existence, even in the midst of evil thoughts and actions. In my worldly thinking, acknowledging Satan seemed awkward because I used to think that people who mentioned the name Satan or spoke of the devil were religious fanatics. But how can we effectively resist what we do not recognize?

Satan is the "father of lies" (John 8:44). As the Word says, lying is his native language. When we sense the presence of those contaminating feelings or feel enticed to do things that are not taught to be right by the Word of God, we can know we are hearing from the enemy. Satan masquerades himself as an angel of light to lure us away from righteousness (2 Corinthians 11:14). What he offers might make sense and sound good, or even promising, but spiritual bondage awaits those who choose his way.

The War

Satan brings havoc into our lives by setting us up to fight against one another. Realize that the sister in your Bible study who always has an answer and tells more about her personal life than you ever wanted to know is not your enemy. The brother who feels compelled to share with you your spiritual shortcomings, as he sees them, every Sunday morning after church is not your enemy. Perhaps these folks were vulnerable because they were not wearing God's armor. Satan grabbed them, and they still do not know who has a hold on them. God would like to win them over, but they must surrender to Him. The annoying and troublesome people in our lives need our prayers—just as we do if we are the annoying and troublesome people in the lives of others!

When we are not covered by Jesus Christ, we lack the discernment to identify that which is of the enemy. This is why it is important to bathe our minds in Christ and His Word and to stand prepared to use Him as our weapon. God's Word teaches us that the weapons of our warfare are not carnal, or of the flesh, but mighty through God (2 Corinthians 10:4). Considering this, in the same manner that a soldier would put on his armor for physical protection, it is wise for us to put on the full spiritual armor of God for spiritual protection.

> Stand firm then, with the belt of truth buckled around your waist, with the breastplate of righteousness in place, and with your feet fitted with the readiness that comes from the gospel of peace. In addition to all this, take up the shield of faith, with which you can extinguish all the flaming arrows of the evil one. Take the helmet of salvation and the sword of the Spirit, which is the word of God. And pray in the Spirit on all occasions with all kinds of prayers and requests. With this in mind, be alert and always keep on praying for all the saints.
> —Ephesians 6:14–18

Let's take a moment to look at each piece of God's armor.

- **Belt of truth**: When we gird ourselves with the belt of truth, we become spiritually mature, with spiritual wisdom and understanding. We will be able to stand firm with the Word as our foundation and not be deceived by the enemy.

- **Breastplate of righteousness**: The breastplate of righteousness allows us to stand upright before God. We stand confidently, knowing we are protected by the righteousness of Jesus Christ. As a result, we can face the enemy without fear or doubt.

- **Shoes of the gospel of peace**: The shoes of the gospel of peace provide us with spiritual peace in the midst of our battles. We are able to walk in agreement with Jesus Christ and follow His example. Our walk is a reflection of the attitude with which we serve.

- **Shield of faith**: The shield of faith encompasses our belief in the power of Jesus Christ as He covers us. We are able to stand up against all the flaming arrows of the enemy because we trust that Jesus is with us and that He has already overcome the world.

- **Helmet of salvation**: The helmet of salvation enables us to think like Christ by washing sin from our minds. It enables us to focus on what is true, honest, just, pure, lovely, and of good report when the enemy tries to lure us toward unrighteousness (Philippians 4:8 KJV).

- **Sword of the Spirit**: The sword of the Spirit, which is the Word of God, will penetrate anything the enemy throws at us. It provides us with light, even when darkness surrounds us.

Satan is powerful, and we in our flesh are weak against him. If we turn to the Lord, He assures us that His strength is made perfect in our weakness (2 Corinthians 12:9). We should not hesitate to claim Jesus' authority and victory over evil forces.

Satan knows the power of Jesus, and if we "resist the devil," "he will flee" (James 4:7).

The war is ongoing. Though my journey has been full of tests and some very unpleasant trials, it is wonderful to know that God has been with me during those times. It is wonderful to know that I do not have to do it all by myself. In whatever I do, even as I write, I am leaning on Jesus.

Time to Reflect

1. What area(s) in your life do you believe Satan is currently attacking?

2. Pray right now for the Lord's help.

> *Dear heavenly Father,*
>
> *Lord, I come to You, acknowledging that You are in control. Please remove anything in my heart that would hinder You from hearing me. Protect me, Lord, in the area(s) of _____. Comfort me in the midst of this (or these) battle(s). Help me to see the truth clearly and not feed on the lies that continually enter my mind. Guard my heart and mind, in the name of Jesus, with the peace of God that transcends all understanding (Philippians 4:7). I offer myself as a living sacrifice, Father. May I learn Your ways, in order that Your will may be done. Thank You, Father, for the changes You are creating in me. Amen.*

3. Write down the names of those you consider to be your enemies. Then acknowledge the role of the real enemy. Next, take a moment and pray for those you consider to be your enemies.

4. Write down the names of those whom the enemy has used you to hurt or contaminate. Consider how you might want someone to become reconciled with you. Then surrender yourself to bringing forth God's glory by doing "to others what you would have them do to you" (Matthew 7:12).

Chapter Ten

Why Me?

No discipline seems pleasant at the time, but painful. Later on, however, it produces a harvest of righteousness and peace for those who have been trained by it.
—Hebrews 12:11

IT IS NOT uncommon for someone to ask God, "Why me?" in the midst of the storms in life. None of us is exempt from experiencing storms, and none of us is alone. Our storm may be a spring shower or a hurricane, but God desires for us to persevere in the race marked out for us (Hebrews 12:1). God created us for Himself, and during any storm, we are still to persevere with praise.

Consider storms to be times of discipline. "No discipline seems pleasant at the time, but painful. Later on, however, it produces a harvest of righteousness and peace for those who have been trained by it" (Hebrews 12:11). So…why not you? Focus on what God does for you, with you, and in you as a result of your storms. Remember, in whatever we are going through, God wants to purge us of the things that hinder us from being holy. Through our hardship, He desires to make us into the individuals He designed us to be. God can take circumstances that were meant for evil and bring good out of them (Genesis 50:20). God demonstrated this principle when Joseph's brothers sold him to the Ishmaelites, who took him to Egypt. God was with Joseph, and therefore everything worked out for Joseph's good and God's glory.

When we are in storms such as divorce, infidelity, abuse, disease, or bereavement, the battle with our flesh can become intense. To overcome our struggles, we have to draw nearer to the Lord so we can hear the direction of the Holy Spirit. We have to walk believing we need God, being careful never to praise ourselves for making it through any storm. When we make it through a storm proclaiming that only God brought us through it, believing He will do it again becomes a little easier. Our faith increases a little more, and in the next storm, we will be able to stand up a little stronger.

Each time we come out of our storms praising God, we mature a little more into the spiritual warriors God desires us to become. Our delight, commendation, exaltation, and reverential awe should be evident in our praise and offered because of who God is, not because of how we feel. How easy it is to praise God when times are good! Our storms provide opportunities in which our faith can be exercised and grow stronger and in which we can learn to praise in all circumstances.

For those who do not know Jesus, these same storms can be debilitating, bringing on feelings of unworthiness, unfairness, blame, failure, fear, shame, resentment, embarrassment, anger, and pride. These people may come out of the storm excessively needy, turning to various people to fill the void or striving for financial and educational success to feel better about themselves. Only God holds the power to use us in these circumstances for His glory and our good. We may not be capable of seeing past our current situation, "but with God all things are possible" (Matthew 19:26).

I know what it is like to be in situations that cause me to hang my head and whisper, "Lord, I do not need this in my life." God knows that if I knew everything I was going to experience before I experienced it, I would have gone to great lengths to avoid those trials. If I did that, however, I would have lost opportunities to exercise my faith. I would have forfeited opportunities to practice

Why Me?

what God's Word instructs me to do. Essentially, I would have chosen to live in darkness, never having witnessed God's power to carry me through.

My marriage, which began in adultery, is one of the areas in which God has revealed Himself most to me. He drew me toward Himself as He allowed me to experience the consequences of sin. He presented me with many opportunities to increase my faith. For the most part, Dan and I work really well in managing our household. He is the kind of man who works selflessly to provide for our family. He shows his undying devotion to our children by spending time with them as often as he can, and his supportiveness toward me still impresses me. However, the initial main ingredients in our union were selfishness and lust. The consequences carved grooves, much like scars on one's skin, into the fabric of our foundation.

Amid the responsibilities of parenting and the daily shuffle of meeting family needs, Dan and I lacked the intimate communication necessary for a healthy marriage. We recognized the distance but seldom discussed it. Both spiritually and in our leisure time, he gravitated one way and I another. Consequently, like a snake, infidelity slithered into our marriage.

At the revelation point, the point at which God brought what was in the dark into the light, I knew God was allowing us to enter into this storm for a reason. I deplored the cloud that was raining on my marriage. I grasped for direction in life. In a calm moment, I asked God what He wanted me to know and what He wanted to do through me. I was eager to know God's answers, because there seemed to be no escaping this storm. It was happening, and I was scared. Life suddenly became dim. Old insecurities of not truly being loved ran full force throughout my body. The aches of my heart stretched to the temples of my head.

A profound moment occurred when I saw a picture of the "other woman." However, I didn't just see a random face—I saw myself in that other woman. I saw the toughness of her heart displayed in the emptiness of her eyes. Oddly, I felt compassion. I imagined the events in her life that could have brought her to the point of willingly becoming a mistress. Cursing her or calling her names, an instinctive response, would do no good. I knew that. I realized this woman did not recognize that her behavior was a reflection of her relationship with God. Attacking her would only bring out the warrior she felt she had to become to protect herself and survive in this world. As mad as I wanted to be, I knew the truth: she was no different than I.

I prayed for restoration in my marriage, but I also contacted a divorce attorney. My thoughts rambled in every direction. However, our pastor agreed to meet with us, and we were forced to look at our relationship in deeper ways than ever before. I knew that through my obedience the end result would be good, but with the intensity of the storm, I struggled with obedience. For this reason, I did not look forward to counseling, and many times my feet felt weighted with lead when we approached the office.

During this ordeal, our pastor left a lasting impression on me. His lack of judgmentalism, coupled with his faith in what God could do in and with our marriage, modeled aspects of Christ for me. Knowing that the Holy Spirit had led us to First Baptist Church, I was sure God was at work during our counseling sessions. God had my attention. My need to grow in my faith in the healing and transforming power of God echoed within me through the Holy Spirit.

Healing was inseparable from pressing toward the Lord. Emotionally, I was brought to a point of exhaustion in front of the Lord. Prayers for my marriage began yielding to my desire to retreat from my marriage. At times divorce still sounded sweeter as I tried to push through this fierce storm. During a moment of silence, after pouring my heart out before the Lord, I heard a whisper from within. I recognized this whisper as the voice of the Holy Spirit revealing to me how much and how long I too had grieved God. Just as a parent watches over a child and is grieved by his or her wrong actions, God, our Father, watches over us. He too reacts to our behaviors and the decisions we, His children, make.

God's revelation brought me to the floor in tears. God's love and grace for me was magnified all at once. He had created me for His purpose, yet I had neglected Him incessantly throughout my life. I hadn't shown love to Him or acknowledged His love for me. Though I gave little thought to pleasing Him, He was at work in my life. Having the power to do all things, He chose to bless me abundantly. He showed His mercy by sparing me from painful consequences of certain choices. He showered me with His grace and entrusted me with the gift of children.

I realized for the first time that my marriage was a ministry. In this storm, God wanted me to show grace toward Dan in the same manner God had shown it to me. He wanted me to pour out onto Dan the love He had poured out onto me. At that point, I embarked on a road of discovery, through God's Word, of what being a wife means to *God*. I was being led to worship the Lord by showing reverence to my husband without condition (Ephesians 5). I was to do *my* part to be holy, to model holiness, and to assist Dan in love, as his helper, to fulfill his potential in Christ. God would do the rest.

I marveled at the difference between my expectations of a wife and God's expectations. God revealed to me that He wanted me to show forth His grace by forgiving both myself and my husband, by respecting my husband, by becoming a prayerful wife, and by committing to my husband's spiritual growth. As a wife, I was to reflect Jesus. My marriage was my faith opportunity.

Reconciliation, which we could only see with God in the midst, became visible. Something new stood out about my husband. I saw a hero in Dan. Transparency had been his hang-up, and for the first time, I saw my husband's heart as he opened up and shared, despite the odds. God's pruning always prepares us for the work He desires to do through us. As Dan opened up before God and before me, God sent men into his life who began to share with him, giving him the opportunity to encourage these men and share with them what God had taught him.

A relationship with the Lord does not prevent us from encountering temptation. However, God's Word teaches us that "there hath no temptation taken you but such as is common to man: but God is faithful, who will not suffer you to be tempted above that ye are able; but will with the temptation also make a way to escape, that ye may be able to bear it" (1 Corinthians 10:13 KJV). There is nothing we have experienced or will experience that is foreign to the rest of God's children. However, Jesus is sovereign in heaven and on earth, and with Him we will be able to bear our experiences. He says so in the verse above.

One of the things I admire about the apostle Paul is his attitude. I cannot imagine that he would ask "why me" in the midst of his storms. He disciplined himself to be content in all circumstances. He welcomed all trials and tribulations and prevailed through them in the name of Jesus. He knew that through trials and tribulations he had the opportunity to increase his spiritual maturity. He learned, whether in abundance or in need, to be content (Philippians 4:11-13). For Jesus' sake Paul took pleasure in storms, so that God would receive the glory through him.

Accepting God's will during our storms increases our faith. God's Word tells us that "faith is being sure of what we hope for and certain of what we do not see" (Hebrews 11:1), and "blessed are those who have not seen and yet have believed" (John 20:29). Blessed are those who have faith. If we intend to walk in the light and show God's glory, then how we get through our storms will be far different than the way the rest of the world faces troubles.

Time to Reflect

1. What has happened in your life that has caused you to ask God, "Why me?"

2. How have these circumstances affected your life?

3. Proverbs 8:32 says, "Blessed are those who keep my ways." Talk to God about your circumstances. Then write down anything He reveals to you about what you have to do before He can use you in or as a result of your trial(s).

4. What has God taught you as a result of your trial(s)?

Chapter Eleven

Adjusting Your Life

> *I have set you an example that you should do
> as I have done for you.*
> —John 13:15

ONCE WE ENTER into a relationship with God and receive revelation from Him, it is time to act accordingly and adjust our lives. This is worship. Jesus walked according to God's counsel in order to bear fruit. He made known to His disciples what He learned from the Father (John 15:15). As Jesus served for the glory of God, He said, "I have set you an example that you should do as I have done for you" (John 13:15). "This is to my Father's glory, that you bear much fruit, showing yourselves to be my disciples" (John 15:8). The Holy Spirit reveals to us what the Father says (John 14:26). As God reveals and teaches truth to us, He is calling us to apply those lessons to our everyday walk, and we in turn should share with others what He has taught us.

Adjusting our lives requires us to live in obedience and with a sense of awareness of the fact that our lives do not belong to us. As we take inventory of relationships with others, considering how they influence our lives and how we influence theirs is pertinent. It may be necessary to distance yourself from relationships that could hinder you from moving in God's direction. It may also be necessary for you to learn how to minister in the relationships you embrace.

Assessing our behavior in daily living is also valuable. As followers of Jesus, our behavior ought to reflect holiness. One thing that keeps people from adjusting their lives according to the direction of God is a desire to excuse existing behavior. As social beings, we acquire many of our behavioral patterns by adopting what we see others do and from reacting to what we experience. We begin to identify ourselves with the behavior, believing what we do is who we are and that we cannot be helped. However stuck in our ways we get, God has the power to transform us. Whatever addictions we battle, God is greater than the source. We welcome God to have His way with us when we begin to obey Him without having all our questions answered. We may not know how, but only that it is possible with God. We may not know why, but only that it is for God's purpose and glory.

Some people fail to adjust their lives because they procrastinate. They choose to put off doing what God has already revealed and called them to do. They decide that when the circumstances are right, when they become more adequate in a certain area, when their spouses join them, when they muster up enough courage, or simply when it's next time, only then will they adjust their lives. This way of thinking causes stagnation—the right circumstances never materialize, they don't develop the skills they think they need, the spouse can't decide, and on it goes. God reveals for a purpose, and the time to adjust our lives is when He reveals. "A time is coming and has now come when the true worshipers will worship the Father in spirit and truth, for they are the kind of worshipers the Father seeks" (John 4:23). The time to adjust your life is now.

God's nature is to pursue us in order to develop a relationship with us, despite our shortcomings. God reveals things to us continually, but if our spiritual eyes are not fixed on Him, we do not always see.

Adjusting Your Life

We live in a world where many people adjust their lives according to their own nature. People lead secret lives, and laws are made in the name of tolerance. Jesus, however, was not of this world. He was pretty special, because He did not fit our mold of normality. He adjusted His life to serve the Father by serving others. He was so focused on what God wanted of Him that He did not waste any time trying to do what others wanted Him to do.

As for us, it can be pretty hard to adjust our lives, because we focus on pleasing parents, spouses, friends, employers, co-workers, children, or neighbors in ways that do not necessarily please God. Jesus served for the purpose of revealing Himself to those the Father enabled to come to Him. He adjusted His life according to the direction of God and acknowledged that He could do nothing without the Father. God was in control.

Jesus directed His disciples to adjust their lives with regard to others. He said, "Love one another. As I have loved you, so you must love one another" (John 13:34). He showed us how to love one another when He washed His disciples' feet. He even washed the feet of the disciple He knew was going to betray Him. How awesome is that? Imagine Jesus washing your feet! What an overwhelming blessing that would be. Jesus did not think of Himself too highly to serve others in this lowly manner of washing feet. Yet, He is Lord. As Jesus did, we too should adjust the attitude with which we interact with others and be willing to serve, even in menial ways. Jesus is the guide for adjusting your life.

The renewal of our minds begins with filling our minds with God's righteousness. He desires to bring us out of this worldly realm and work through each of us. God's Word teaches us that others will know we are followers of Jesus if we love one another (John 13:35). How we relate to one another is a testimony of our relationship with God.

Since we live in this world, it is unrealistic not to expect some opposition when we are genuine in our walk with Jesus. As we fill our minds with God's righteousness, it will soon manifest itself in our behavior. Friends may be lost and others distanced, yet new, Christ-centered ones will follow.

After learning that I needed to adjust my life, I began praying fervently for guidance about a situation I had faced. I knew God was revealing truth to me when I learned about Jesus serving His disciples by washing their feet. I asked the Lord specifically how I could serve someone I had sinned against. Answers to my prayers lit up during my Bible study time. I was clearly led to do something I would never have dreamed of doing. But I found myself not ready to adjust in a certain manner and afraid to serve in the way I was being led to serve. Then I received my last confirmation of what I was to do while I was reading *The Purpose Driven Life* by Rick Warren. I closed this book spiritually awakened and could not continue reading it until I did what the Lord was telling me to do.

Well, I could have walked away and never finished the book, but before starting it I had made a personal commitment to complete this book for the sake of my spiritual growth in Christ. Therefore, I had to explore what God was placing on my heart.

God's Word tells us to confess our sins to each other and pray for each other so we may be healed (James 5:17). This requires faith and obedience. We are also instructed not to simply listen to the Word, but to do what it says, because if our faith is not accompanied by action, then it is dead (James 1:22; 2:17). Just like a child becoming an adult, when we know better, we are expected to do better. Our obedience to God's Word impacts not only our relationship with God, but also the lives of those around us. Lives are impacted because our obedience brings forth God's glory, and God's power and essence are seen in His glory.

In the midst of my desire to be obedient to God's Word, I felt as if I were another person. I knew I would never have done what I did of my own accord, but that the Holy Spirit was leading me. I was led to express my deep sympathy and confess to a woman that during her marriage I had permitted a three-month affair to occur. I was startled by this clear revelation and spent some more time communing with my Father.

In my carnal nature I experienced fear. I shared my intentions with another woman, and she prompted many discouraging "what if she does this or that" questions and "I don't see why you feel you have to contact her; I wouldn't" statements. I was aware that Satan was trying to change my mind.

We may not understand where the Lord is leading us, but He expects us to obey. I had no idea where He was leading me, but as this friend tried to dissuade me, a Scripture verse came to mind: "In all things God works for the good of those who love him, who have been called according to his purpose" (Romans 8:28). There was no turning back now. I had to act, or else my unwillingness to let God have His way would be etched in my brain forever. God's Word tells us that "fools mock at making amends for sin, but goodwill is found among the upright" (Proverbs 14:9). I had to ignore my own hindering thoughts and the hindering thoughts of this friend.

It took a while for me to make contact with this woman, and with each failed attempt I thought about stopping. I would tell myself, "At least I tried," and "If she has caller ID, I don't want her to think I'm stalking her." But this was not about what she or anyone else thought. It was about my relationship with the Lord. It was about serving others in the Lord. It was about blessing others.

We are to do whatever *we can do* to make amends, to serve others as Jesus did, and to show God's love. There is no guarantee that all things will be resolved in the manner in which we expect. However, just as God deals with us, He will deal with others. I expected all things would work out for my good because God's Word tells me they will. Since I had the ability to keep trying to contact her, I did.

Despite my fear, my desire to grow in Christ remained fervent. My eyes were on the Lord and nowhere else. In His timing, I finally spoke with the woman. Her tense demeanor softened, and she seemed flabbergasted as I expressed what the Lord had placed on my heart toward her unspoken needs. As difficult as that experience was for me, I was overwhelmingly blessed. After refraining from obedience initially, the woman contacted me later the same day and admitted that she wanted to be obedient to the Lord as I was, and asked if she could pray for me. (To say she wanted to be anything like *me* was profound for me and bold for her.) She prayed for me.

Now this was *only* the work of the Lord. Thank You, Jesus. "What is impossible with men is possible with God" (Luke 18:27). The adjustments needed in your life to reach all possibilities are through the molding hand of God. He has a purpose for you no matter your circumstance.

Time to Reflect

1. When you consider how to adjust your life, what does Matthew 6:33 teach you to do first?

2. In what ways have you conformed to this world?

3. Pray for God's help to renew your mind and the standards by which you live.

> *Dear heavenly Father,*
>
> *I desire to change my way of living. I ask in the name of Jesus for You to replace my ignorance with truth. I especially need help with _____. Please forgive me, Father, for falling short in this area. Give me a discerning spirit to know the difference between Your ways and everyone else's ways. Open my eyes, Lord, that I might live in this world but not be of this world. Bring into captivity every thought to the obedience of Christ. Thank You for helping me to know that I need to change. Amen.*

Adjusting Your Life

4. In what ways is God leading you to adjust your life?

5. It is a matter of choice. Will you choose to adjust your life in the areas God is calling you to change right now?

www.ingramcontent.com/pod-product-compliance
Lightning Source LLC
Chambersburg PA
CBHW060341080526
44584CB00013B/860